Solo and Duet Books

For the Piano

Collected and Harmonized,
Edited and Fingered
by ANGELA DILLER
and ELIZABETH QUAILE

FIRST SOLO BOOK
New Edition

SECOND SOLO BOOK
New Edition

THIRD SOLO BOOK

FOURTH SOLO BOOK

FIRST DUET BOOK

SECOND DUET BOOK
New Edition

→ THIRD DUET BOOK

ED 1440
ISBN 0-634-00775-0

G. SCHIRMER, *Inc.*

DISTRIBUTED BY

HAL•LEONARD®
CORPORATION

7777 W. BLUEMOUND RD. P.O. BOX 13819 MILWAUKEE, WI 53213

PREFACE

This Series has two objects:

(1) To provide, in the earliest stages of the child's piano study, material of permanent *musical value* which shall serve as a basis for the development of his taste.

With the exception of a few preliminary exercises, all the pieces in the Series are either folk-tunes that have been sung by generations of children, or classics that should be part of every child's musical experience.

We believe that the child can be interested very early in his musical career in different styles of composition, so we have used folk-tunes of many nations, modal tunes, chorales, etc., including, from the beginning, pieces of irregular metrical structure, i.e., not confined to the usual two- and four-measure phrase-lengths.

Music of this character cannot be heard too often, and we feel sure that the teacher as well as the pupil will appreciate the absence of original "teaching pieces."

(2) To provide a plentiful selection of pieces of real musical interest so carefully graded, both musically and technically, that the child is stimulated but not overtaxed.

The pieces are printed only in the more common major and minor keys, but the child should be taught to transpose the pieces into all keys. This insures a familiarity with the keyboard and a sense of tone-relationship that is invaluable.

In the pieces where dots are first introduced, the dots are printed in that part of the measure where they occur rhythmically. For example, in Number 22, second measure, the "eighth-dot" comes on the first part of the second beat, and is printed in the space where a note on the second beat would be printed. For further illustration, in Number 27, second measure, the dot represents the sixth eighth, and is similarly printed where the note would be; in Number 41, third measure, the dot is printed exactly above the third quarter-note in the bass, with which it agrees rhythmically.

In 6/8 meter, if a note is to be held for an entire measure, it is written

♩. ♩. , *not* ♩: , because the former way indicates more clearly to the eye a measure composed of *two* groups of three eighth-notes.

Further on, the usual form of notation is used.

The slur , dot •, and dots and slur signify *legato, staccato,* and *portamento*, respectively. The mark | means that there is a slight break in the sense, and is used much as a comma is used in punctuating English. The brace indicates the length of the phrase, and is used to aid intelligent reading. The brace does *not* refer to *legato* or *staccato*. For example:

means that the notes are to be played portamento;

means that the notes are to be played staccato.

There are often several ways of phrasing a passage, but since an inexperienced child usually reads from bar to bar, irrespective of the rhythmic grouping of the piece, these indications of one way of phrasing may not be superfluous.

The three books of Duets are graded so as to be used in conjunction with the three books of Solos—although each set is complete in itself.

The necessary foundation for the artistic playing of any instrument is a musical ear. Pianoforte-playing in itself cannot, by any means, be relied upon to furnish this, as the attention of the child is necessarily focused upon the overcoming of technical difficulties. Therefore, it is recommended that the child be given a large experience of music before he begins the study of an instrument. Just as language is learned first by hearing and then by speaking and reading, so music should be learned by experiencing it before learning to read or to perform on an instrument. Singing is the natural mode of musical expression, and learning to sing a large number of good songs "by ear" will greatly broaden the child's musical horizon. When he thus has had actual experience of music, he will be more interested in learning to read and to play.

Thanks are due to Mr. Thomas Whitney Surette, who suggested the writing of this set of books.

ANGELA DILLER
ELIZABETH QUAILE

THE DILLER-QUAILE SERIES
GRADE III

The following books and pieces provide a variety of correlated material for the Third Grade, comprising piano solos, duets, studies in sight-reading and in musical form, song books, theory and keyboard harmony books, and an opera story.

THIRD SOLO BOOK

Pieces for the student's third year, including easy classics and folk-tunes delightfully arranged. Much of the book is made up of attractive pieces by Handel, Haydn, Mozart, Beethoven, Grieg, Schumann, etc. Note the care with which the phrasing is indicated. This makes reading easy and rapid, and helps the pupil to an immediate understanding of the *sense* of the composition.

THIRD DUET BOOK

This book is made up chiefly of pieces by the great masters—pieces which, although their difficulty is kept within very moderate limits, are so lovely in themselves, and arranged with such taste and musicianship, that two adults might easily play through the entire book with great pleasure.

A BAKER'S DOZEN—A method of teaching sight-reading.

This book contains thirteen pieces to read at sight with suggestions as to how you do it. The basic principle is that of seeing the highlights first, and playing them in time no matter what happens. Gradually the pupil adds details until finally he is playing the complete piece.

RHYME AND REASON—15 Piano Pieces.

Each piece in the book specially illustrates one significant point that occurs frequently in the structure of a musical composition, such as plagal cadence, sequence, suspension, organ point and the like. Each piece is preceded by a page of further illustration and definition of the point discussed.

DILLER-PAGE SONG BOOKS, Volumes I and II.

Each volume contains 30 familiar songs to play and sing, including patriotic songs, college songs, folk-songs, and Gilbert & Sullivan written in easy keys appropriate for home and community singing. The pieces also provide excellent material for sight reading. They are useful in furnishing variety in pupils' recitals, the audience joining in singing the familiar tunes.

FIRST THEORY BOOK

While the subject matter of all elementary theory books is the same, this book's distinction is in the care and wisdom that have been applied to the *presentation* of that subject matter, and the detail with which the pupil's work is laid out in exercises. The book covers elements of rhythm, phrasing, meter, major and minor scales, and simple chords and their relations, and lays great stress on thorough and consistent ear-training.

KEYBOARD MUSIC STUDY, Book I.

This book is written with the purpose of giving students practical, first-hand experience of how music is made, not by theorizing about it, but by immediately making it. Using at first a simple vocabulary of "melodic idioms" the student learns to play chords and make melodies on the keyboard. The melodies are then decorated with passing-notes, changing-notes, and appoggiaturas. Each point studied is illustrated with a wealth of quotations from the great composers. Many suggestions for analyzing and memorizing music are given.

STORY OF LOHENGRIN

The opera-story is retold in simple language for children, with easy piano arrangements of the principal musical motives. At the end of the book are musicianly piano arrangements of four important scenes from the opera, including the famous Bridal Chorus. They familiarize the student with more or less extended portions of the music, and at the same time show what use is made of the motives identified in the course of the story.

SHEET MUSIC   Exaudet's Minuet   Sir Pantaloon
                        March of the Three Kings   March of the Musketeers

The Star-Spangled Banner (in B-flat and A-flat). Every pianist should be able to play the National Anthem. The piece is printed in two keys. An essay on the origin of the words and music is included.

A complete list of Diller-Quaile material for *all grades* is printed on the back cover of this book.

CONTENTS

30600c

Third Duet Book

SECONDO

The Heavens are telling

The heavens are telling the Lord's endless glory,
 Through all the earth His praise is found;
The seas reëcho the marvellous story:
 O man, repeat that glorious sound!

The starry host He orders and measures,
 He fills the morning's golden springs,
The sun He wakens from night-curtained slumbers:
 O man, adore the King of kings!

Ludwig van Beethoven

30600 c

Third Duet Book

PRIMO

The Heavens are telling

The heavens are telling the Lord's endless glory,
   Through all the earth His praise is found;
The seas reëcho the marvellous story:
   O man, repeat that glorious sound!

The starry host He orders and measures,
   He fills the morning's golden springs,
The sun He wakens from night-curtained slumbers:
   O man, adore the King of kings!

Ludwig van Beethoven

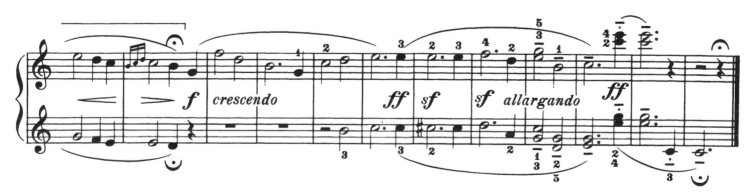

The Little Red Lark

O swan of slenderness,
   Dove of tenderness,
Jewel of joys, arise!
   The little red lark
   Like a soaring spark
Of song to his sunburst flies.
	But till thou'rt risen,
	   Earth is a prison
	Full of my lonesome sighs;
	   Then awake and discover
	   To thy fond lover
	The morn of thy matchless eyes!

Irish Folk-Tune

The Little Red Lark

O swan of slenderness,
Dove of tenderness
Jewel of joys, arise!
The little red lark
Like a soaring spark
Of song to his sunburst flies.

But till thou'rt risen,
Earth is a prison
Full of my lonesome sighs;
Then awake and discover
To thy fond lover
The morn of thy matchless eyes!

Irish Folk-Tune

Gathering Peascods

Allegro

English Country-Dance

30600

Gathering Peascods

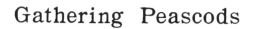

Allegro

English Country-Dance

(Pupil)

3

Le Carnaval
Sarabande

Jean-Baptiste de Lully

Lento

(Pupil)

4

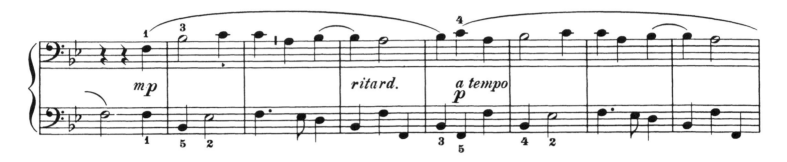

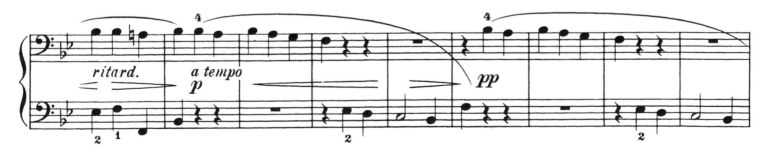

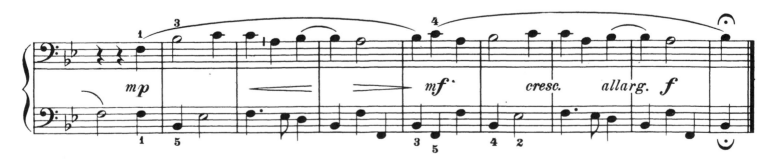

30600

Le Carnaval
Sarabande

Jean-Baptiste de Lully

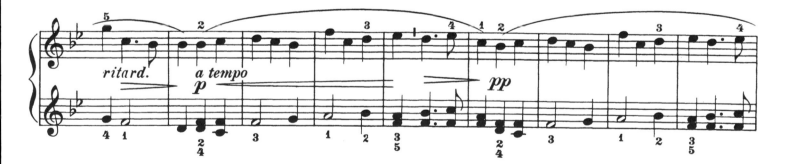

30600

Alle Menschen müssen sterben

Chorale

J. S. Bach

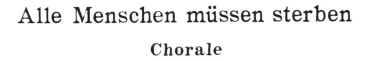

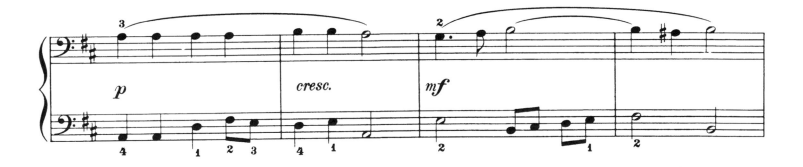

Alle Menschen müssen sterben

Chorale

J. S. Bach

Wandering

To wander is the miller's joy,
    To wander!
To wander is the miller's joy,
    To wander!
He must a wretched miller be
Who never cares the world to see:
    To wander, to wander!
    To wander, to wander!

Franz Schubert

Andante con moto

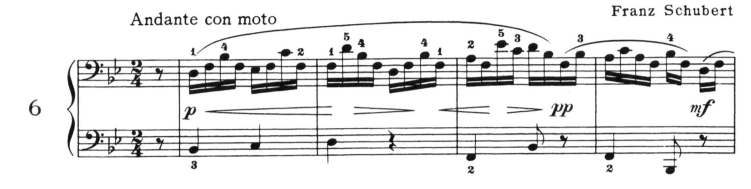

Wandering

To wander is the miller's joy,
    To wander!
To wander is the miller's joy,
    To wander!
He must a wretched miller be
Who never cares the world to see:
    To wander, to wander!
    To wander, to wander!

Andante con moto

Franz Schubert

(Pupil)

6

Idyl

Fr. Černý

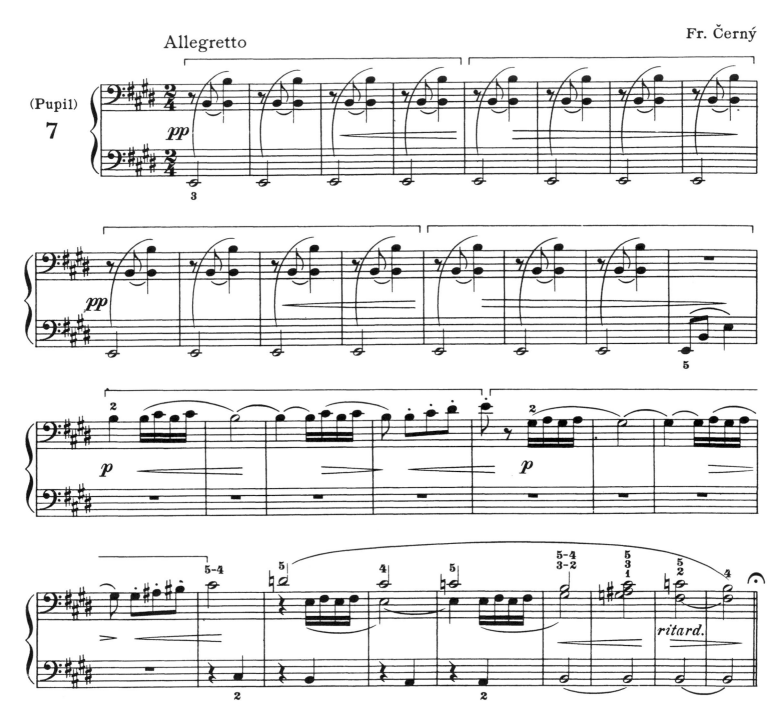

Idyl

Allegretto

Fr. Černý

Wha wadna fecht for Charlie?

Wha wadna fecht for Charlie?   Think on Scotia's ancient heroes,
Wha wadna draw the sword?   Think on foreign foes repell'd,
Wha wadna up and rally   Think on glorious Bruce and Wallace,
At the royal Prince's word?   Who the proud usurpers quell'd!

Wha wadna fecht for Charlie?
Wha wadna draw the sword?
Wha wadna up and rally
At the royal Prince's word?

Scotch Folk-Tune

Marziale

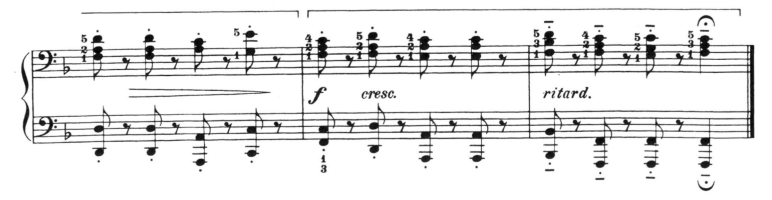

Wha wadna fecht for Charlie?

Wha wadna fecht for Charlie?
Wha wadna draw the sword?
Wha wadna up and rally
At the royal Prince's word?

Think on Scotia's ancient heroes,
Think on foreign foes repell'd
Think on glorious Bruce and Wallace,
Who the proud usurpers quell'd!

Wha wadna fecht for Charlie?
Wha wadna draw the sword?
Wha wadna up and rally
At the royal Prince's word?

Marziale

Scotch Folk-Tune

(Pupil)
8

Waltz

Robert Schumann

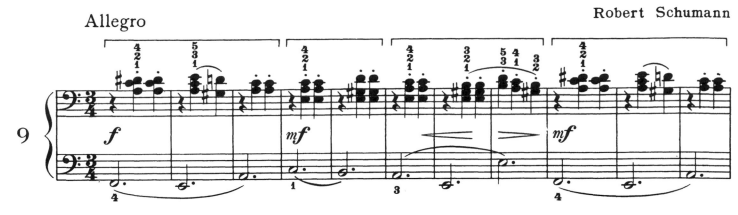

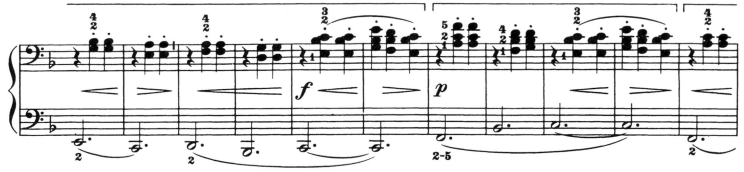

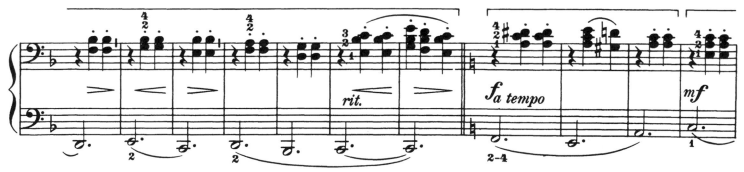

Waltz

Allegro

Robert Schumann

(Pupil) 9

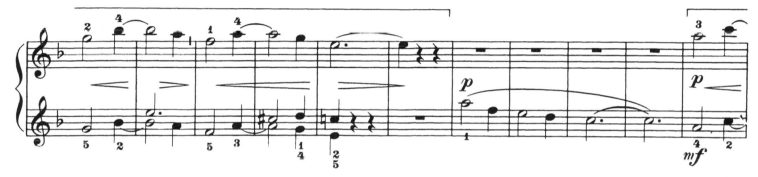

Andante from Symphony
"La Reine de France"

Josef Haydn

10

Andante from Symphony
"La Reine de France"

Josef Haydn

(Pupil)
10

80600

Schwesterlein

German Folk-Tune

Andante con moto

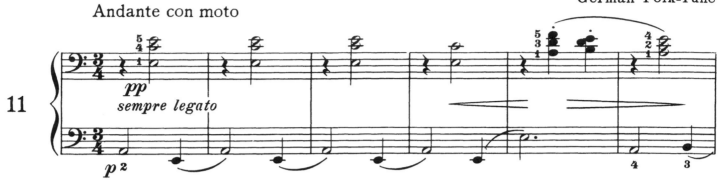

Schwesterlein

German Folk-Tune

Andante con moto

(Pupil)

11

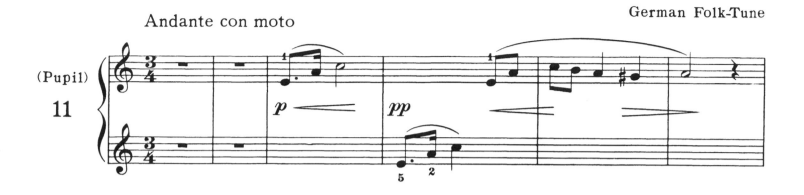

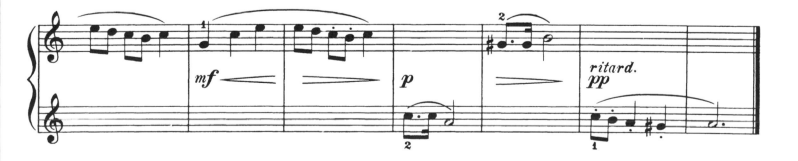

Alla Polka

Vivace

Fr. Černý

(Pupil)

12

Alla Polka

Fr. Černý

12

30600

Venez, agréable Printemps

Allegretto   Old French Melody

(Pupil)

13

Venez, agréable Printemps

Old French Melody

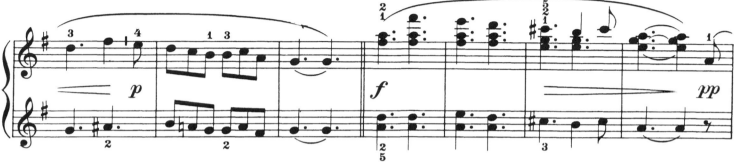

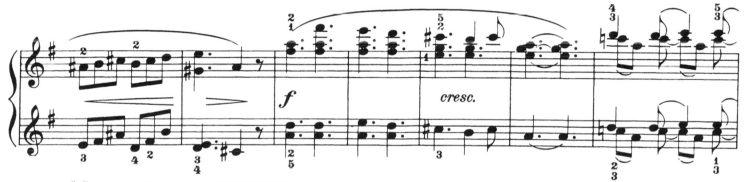

Thou hast left me ever, Jamie

Thou hast left me ever, Jamie,
Thou hast left me ever!
Thou hast left me ever, Jamie,
Thou hast left me ever!
Often thou hast vowed that Death
Only us should sever;
Now thou'st left thy lass for ay –
I shall see thee never, Jamie,
I shall see thee never!

Scotch Folk-Tune

Adagio

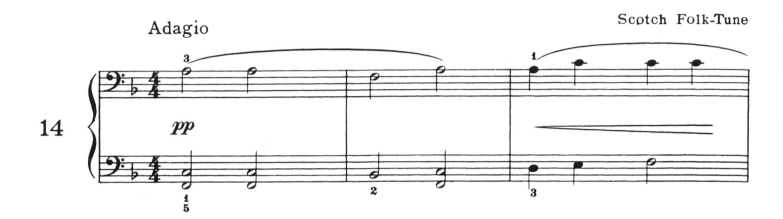

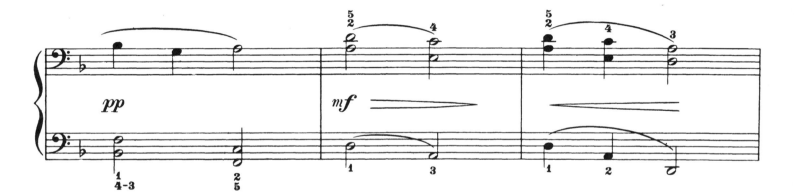

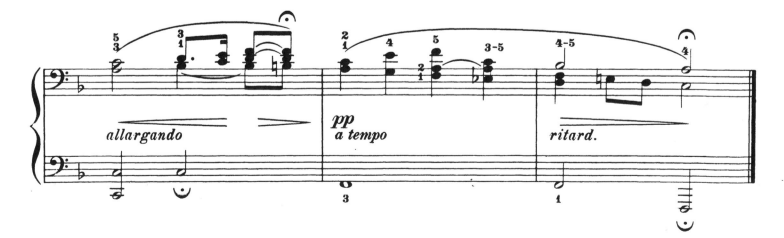

30600

Thou hast left me ever, Jamie

Thou hast left me ever, Jamie,
Thou hast left me ever!
Thou hast left me ever, Jamie,
Thou hast left me ever!
Often thou hast vowed that Death
Only us should sever;
Now thou'st left thy lass for ay –
I shall see thee never, Jamie,
I shall see thee never!

Scotch Folk-Tune

Adagio

(Pupil)

14

The First Primrose

O take, O take, thou child of Spring,
  This Spring's first tender flower,
Despise it not, that later on
  Fair roses June will shower.

The Summer has its golden charm,
  In Autumn hearts are gay;
But Spring is lovelier than all,
  The time of love and play.

For thee and me, O dearest maid,
  The light of Spring is glowing;
Then take the flow'r and rapture yield,
  Thyself on me bestowing.

Edvard Grieg

Allegretto

15

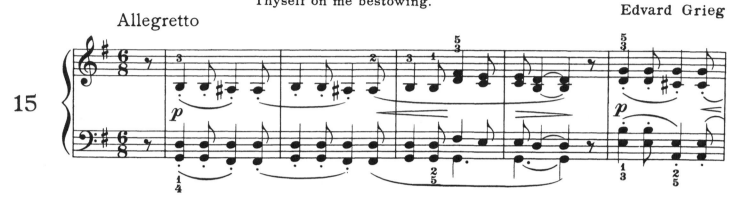

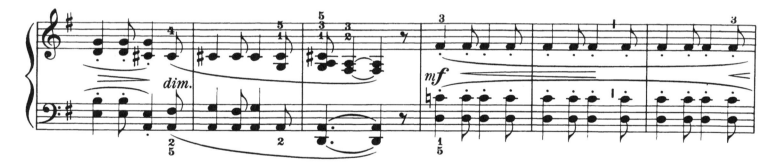

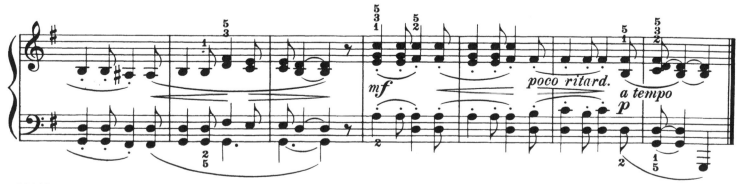

The First Primrose

O take, O take, thou child of Spring,
  This Spring's first tender flower,
Despise it not, that later on
  Fair roses June will shower.

The Summer has its golden charm,
  In Autumn hearts are gay;
But Spring is lovelier than all,
  The time of love and play.

For thee and me, O dearest maid,
  The light of Spring is glowing;
Then take the flow'r and rapture yield,
  Thyself on me bestowing.

Edvard Grieg

Allegretto

(Pupil)

15

30600

Albumleaf

Robert Schumann

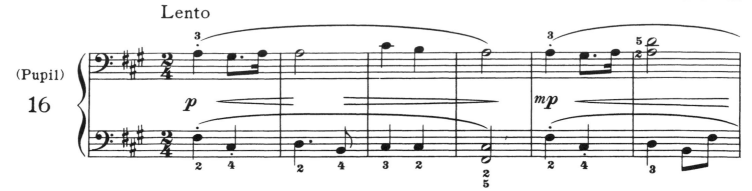

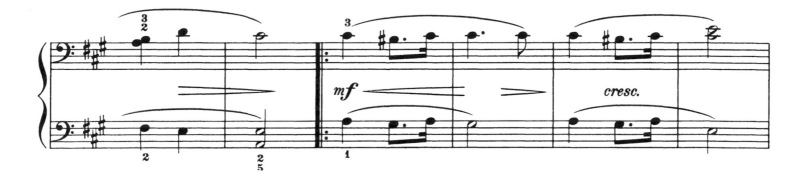

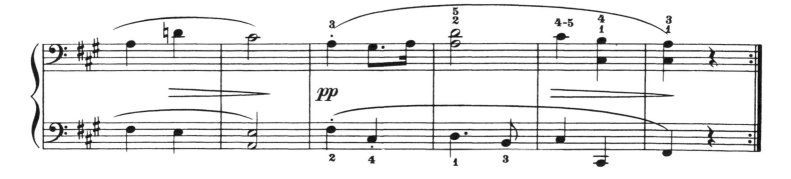

Albumleaf

Robert Schumann

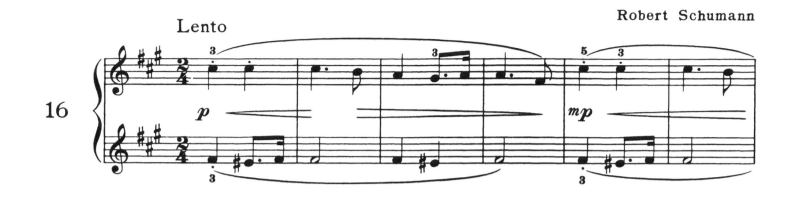

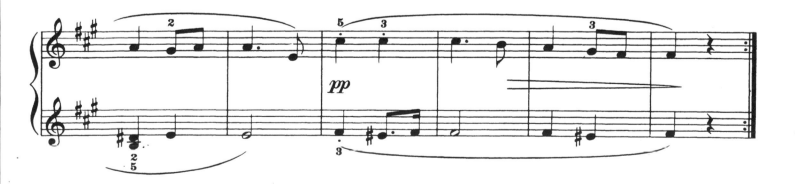

Waltzes

Franz Schubert

Franz Schubert

No. 1

(Pupil)

17

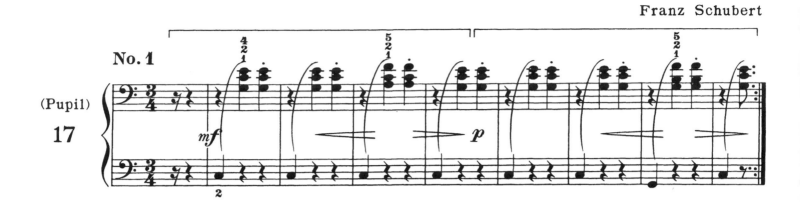

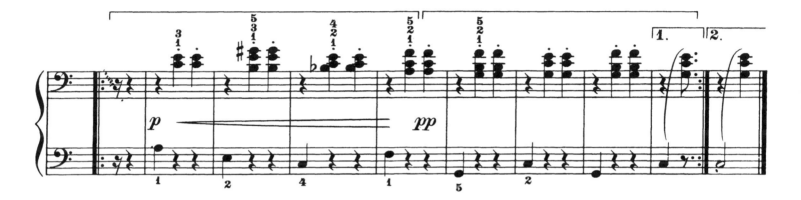

No. 2

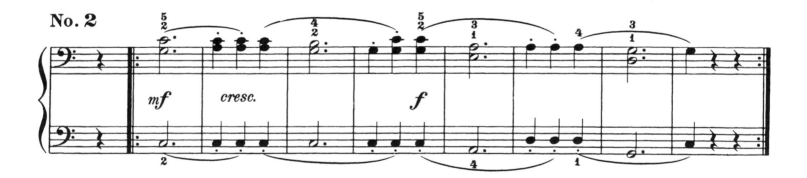

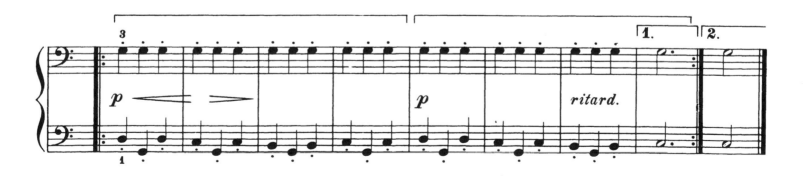

Waltzes

Franz Schubert

No. 1

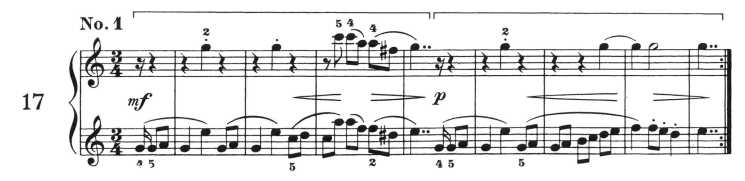

17

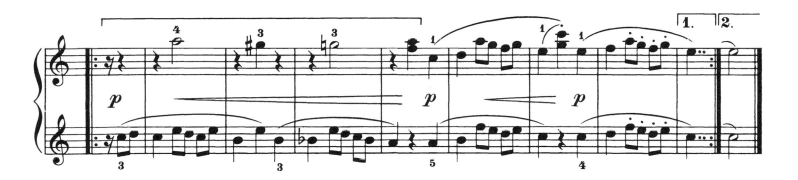

No. 2

30600

No. 3

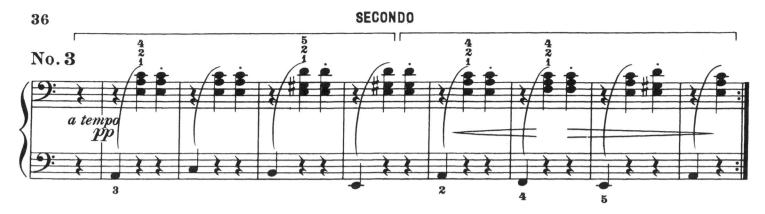

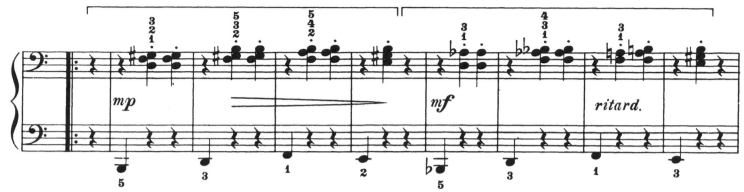

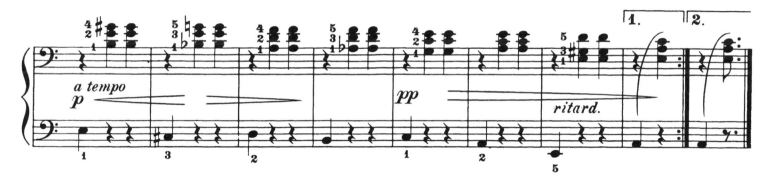

No. 4

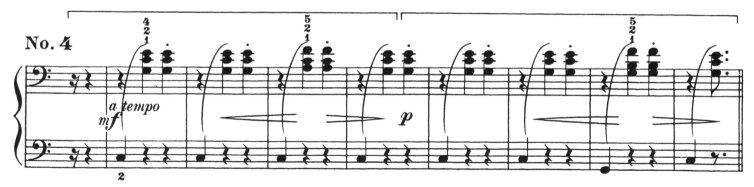

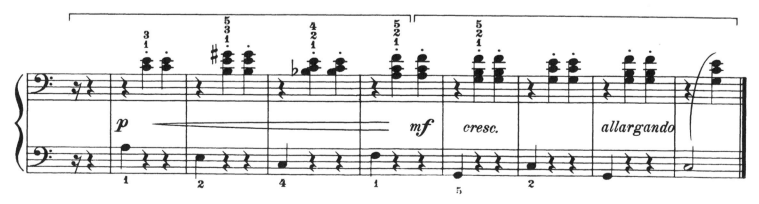

No. 3

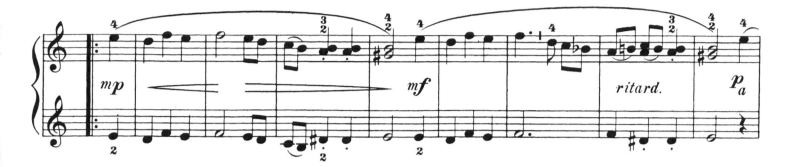

No. 4

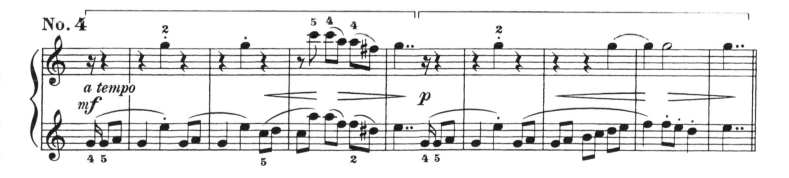

Finnish Folk-Tune

Andante

18

80600

Finnish Folk-Tune

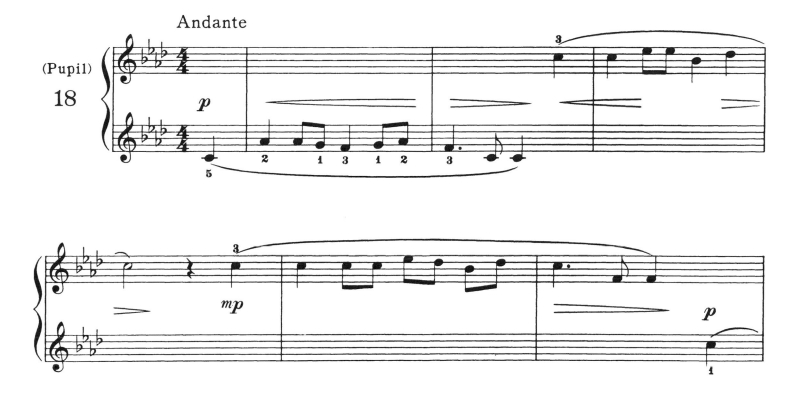

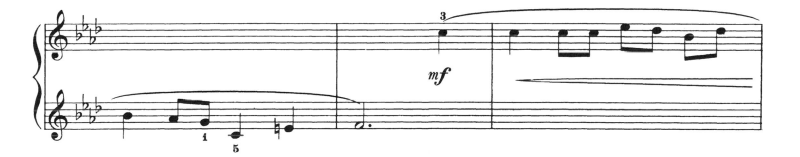

Tambourin

François-Joseph Gossec

(Pupil)
19

Tambourin

François-Joseph Gossec

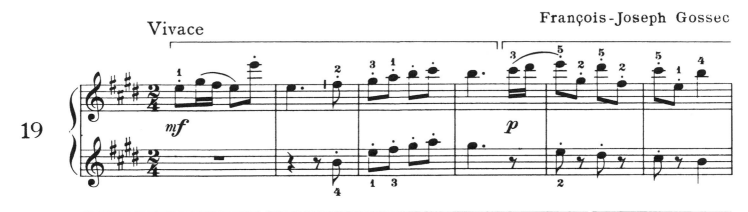

30600

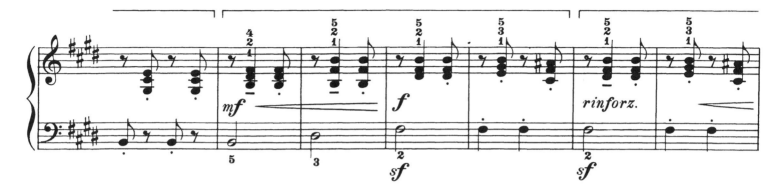

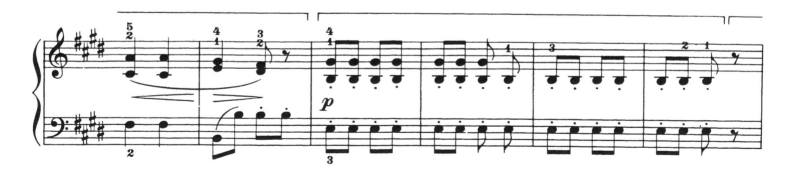

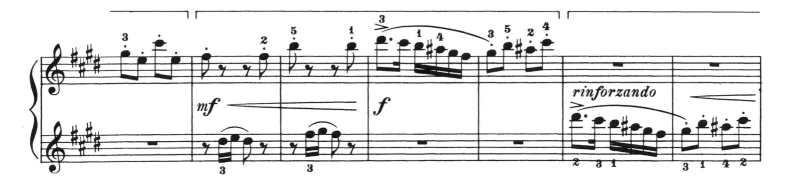

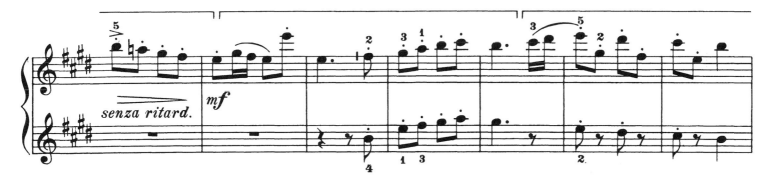

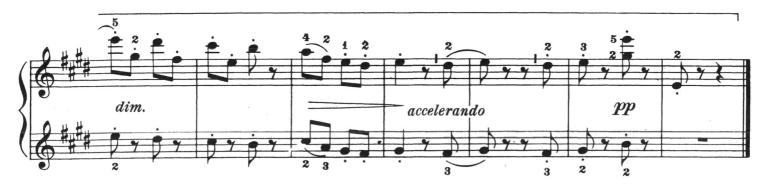

Gavotte
From French Suite No. 5

J. S. Bach

Allegro

(Pupil)

20

30600

Gavotte
From French Suite No. 5

J. S. Bach

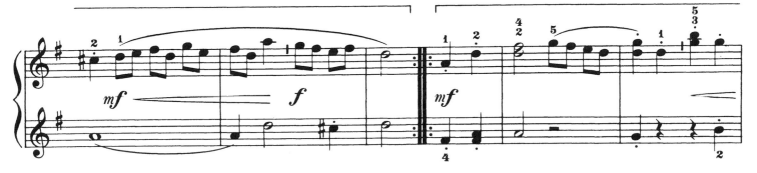

30600

Sarabande
From French Suite No. 1

J. S. Bach

Adagio

(Pupil)

21

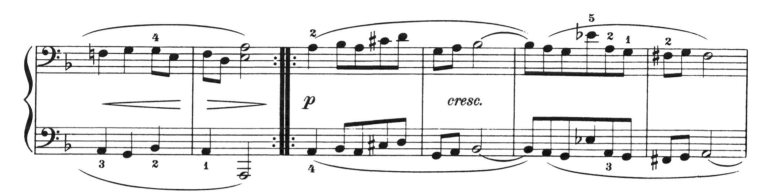

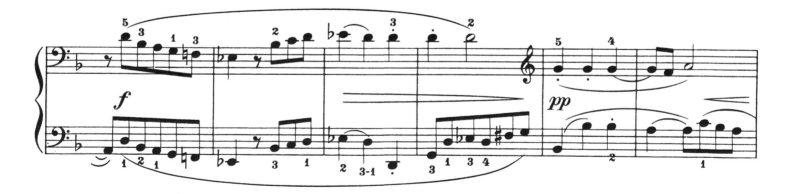

Sarabande
From French Suite No.1

J. S. Bach

Adagio

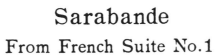

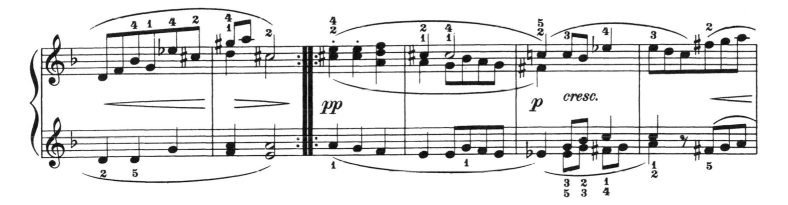

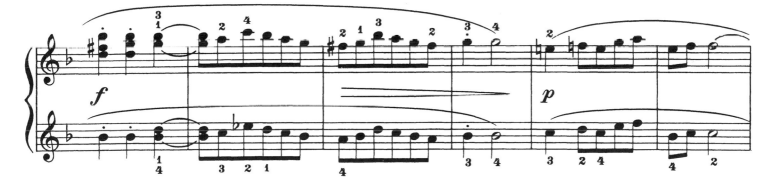

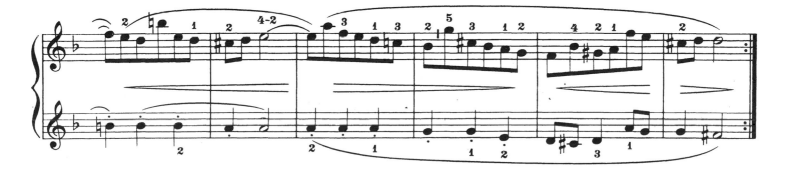

Gavotte

François-Joseph Gossec

Allegretto

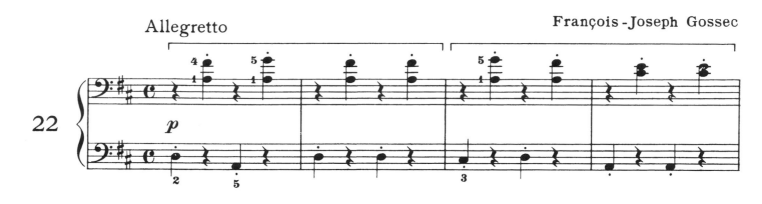

Gavotte

Allegretto

François-Joseph Gossec

SECONDO

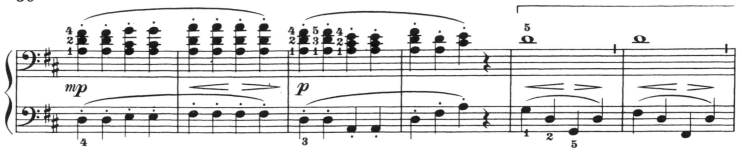

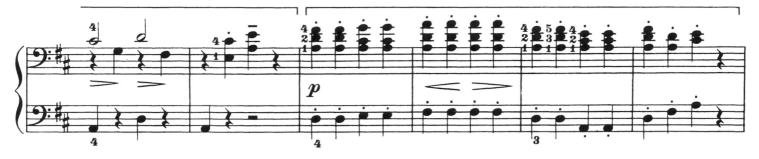

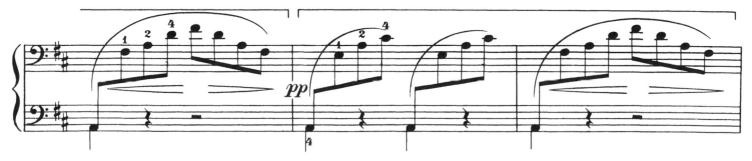

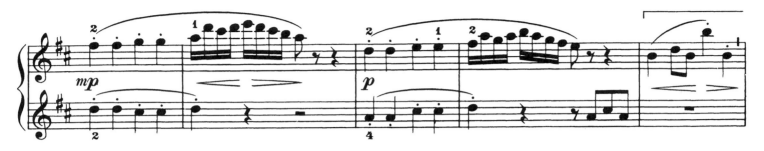

Tempo I°

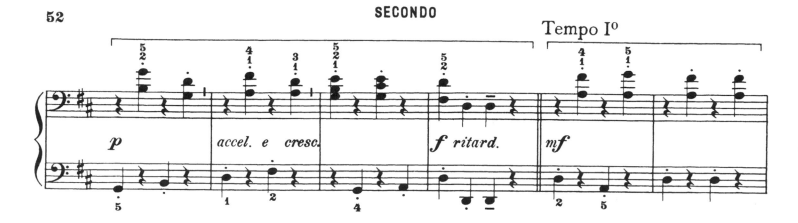

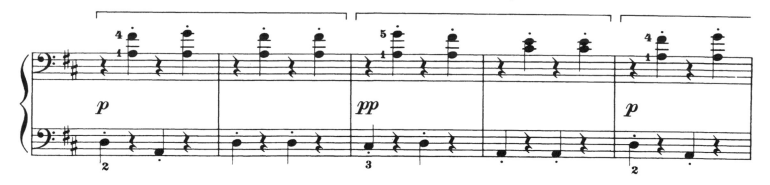

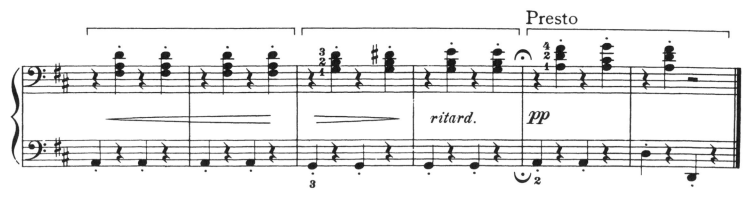

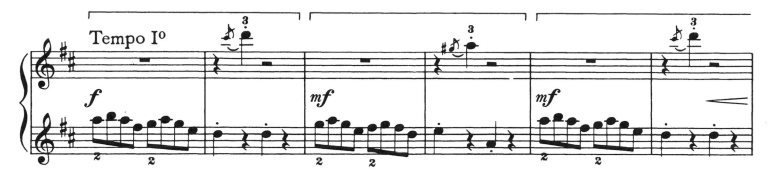

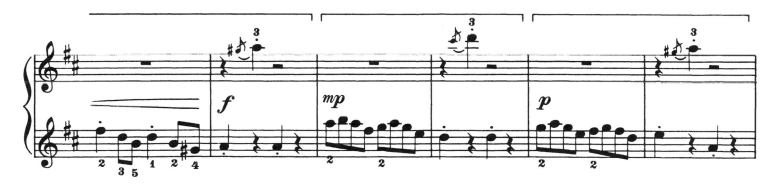

Pastheen Fionn

Oh, fair Pastheen is my heart's delight,
Her gay heart laughs in her blue eye bright,
Like apple-blossoms her bosom white,
And her neck like the swan's on a March morn bright.

Then Oro, will you come with me, come with me, come with me,
Oro, will you come with me, brown girl sweet?
And oh, I would go through snow and sleet,
If you would but come with me, brown girl sweet!

Andante con moto

Irish Folk-Tune

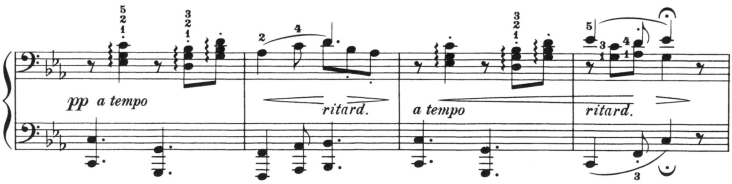

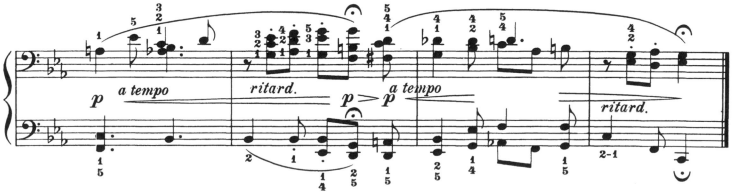

30600

Pastheen Fionn

Oh, fair Pastheen is my heart's delight,
Her gay heart laughs in her blue eye bright,
Like apple-blossoms her bosom white,
And her neck like the swan's on a March morn bright.

Then Oro, will you come with me, come with me, come with me,
Oro, will you come with me, brown girl sweet?
And oh, I would go through snow and sleet,
If you would but come with me, brown girl sweet!

Irish Folk-Tune

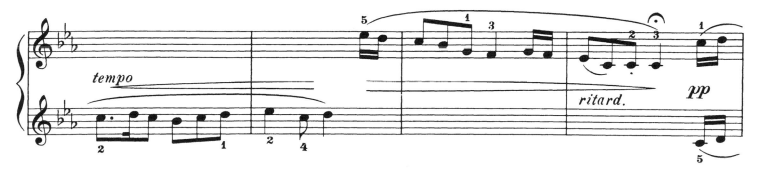

Écossaises

Allegro

Ludwig van Beethoven

(Pupil)
24

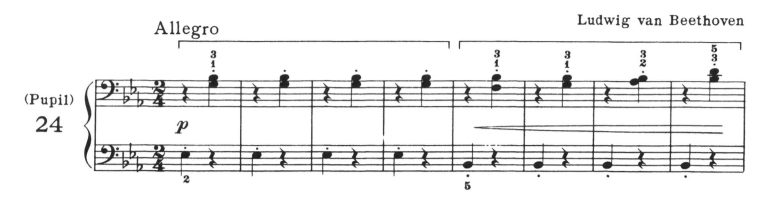

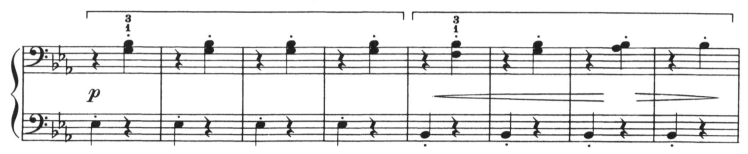

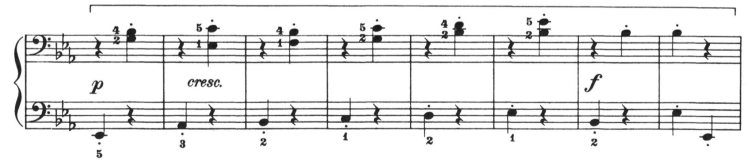

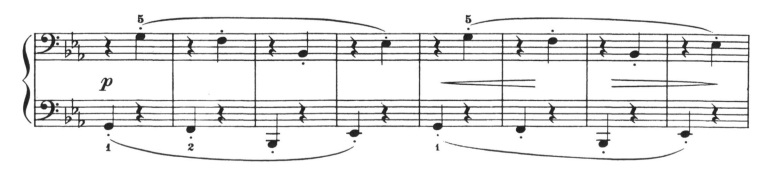

Écossaises

Allegro

Ludwig van Beethoven

24

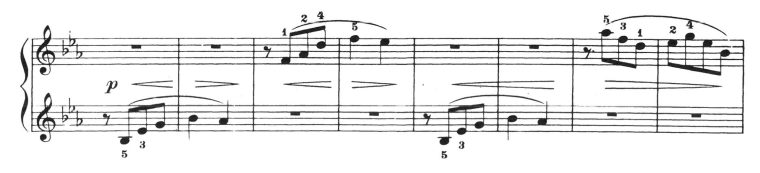

left hand over

SECONDO

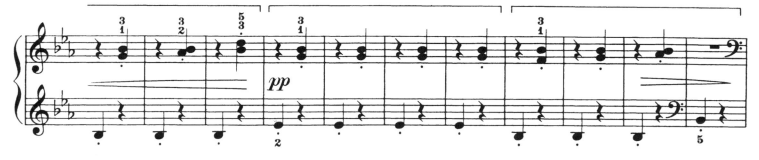

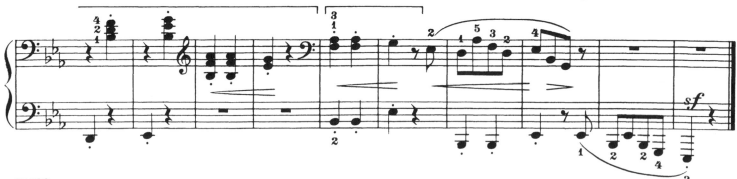

right hand

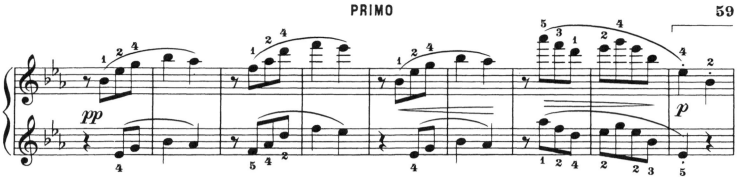

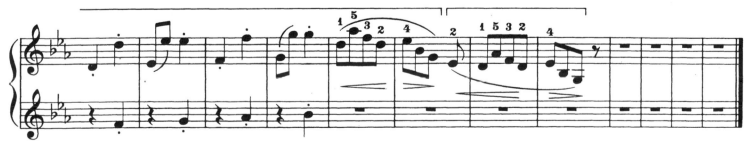

3060